DISCLAIMER

By reading this disclaimer, you fully accept the terms of this disclaimer. If you are not in agreement with this disclaimer, please do not order or read this book. The content of this book is provided for information and educational purposes only. Kindly do not interpret this book or its content for a medication or product. This is only a book guide.

Thanks.

Table of Contents

INTRODUCTION

Gardening has long been accepted as not only a good way to provide relaxation and a sense of pride to the gardener, but also as nourishment that can be for the whole family. Growing grapes is also a great type of gardening that benefits everybody. For the kids it can be some of the best jam they have ever tasted spread across their toast for breakfast. For the adults, grapes can create some of the most delicious wine that has crossed your palate, including that stuff from the store that costs upwards of twenty or thirty dollars a bottle. And remember there is always the sweet taste of satisfaction that comes from growing it yourself.

Planting grapes, whether in your backyard or in a huge vineyard, rewards you with so many things. This is the reason why more and more people make this as their hobby, or even their business. But to be successful, you have to know basic tips for grape planting. Gardening and other vigorous activities promote wellness and normal blood flow in your body, so if you're a senior or a stay at home, growing grapes in your home is a worthwhile hobby. And of course, if your grape vine thrives and is healthy, you can enjoy grapes for free and sometimes sell your surplus harvest to the nearest local market. Here are some great tips for growing grapes effectively.

The first fact that you have to know is that there are certain grape species that can only thrive in certain climates that are appropriate for growing that kind of grape species. You may want to plant Chardonnay and Riesling grapes and dream of producing white wine, but if you are in Florida, that would be impossible. Riesling and Chardonnay are species under Vitis Vinifera, a grape species which requires a long hot season and mild winter. North American countries, France and Luxembourg may be grape-growing countries but Auxerrois (a grape variety that produces a fruity taste) can only be grown in Luxembourg and Canada. Barbera, which has a tarry flavor, can only be grown in Italy and California. There are sites that are dedicated just to giving you detailed descriptions of grape species for growing grapes effectively.

Before getting started, you should know that growing grapes is also like taking care of an infant. Grapes need plenty of sunlight and lots of care. After choosing the type of grapes, check the site and location of your yard whether it has ample sunlight for growing grapes. Competition for sunlight from other taller trees and plants will make your vines sickly. Sunlight is still one of the natural fighters of fungi and other viruses that will attack your grape vines. Check for taller building structures that may hinder sunlight from coming in your yard. Grapes grown with sufficient sunlight are much juicier and better tasting then those grown in dark areas.

The type of soil and its mineral content are also factors in growing grapes. The soil should neither be too moist nor too dry. It should also have the characteristic of not holding water in its particles. It's advised to till the soil first before planting any grape root stock. Check and remove broken bottles and other non-biodegradable materials in the soil. Also remove weeds and stray shrubs in your garden. Weeds will only compete for soil nutrients that your grapes need for growth. Because the roots of your grape vines will extend deeper in the ground, removing boulders and other stones will also be helpful. Also, make sure that in growing grapes, the soil does not appear to be eroding as this will only remove the soil mineral content.

After sometime, your grape vines will start growing sturdy branches. Thus, there is a need to create reliable trellises and a good fence that will block the vines from further crawling outside your yard. To prevent thicker and longer vines, it is better to prune your vines regularly, probably in the months of February and March. If grape vines are in good positions, one can be certain that they will last until harvest. The best time to harvest your grapes is during an early frost. The cold weather helps preserve the grapes so that they will last longer and unharmed. With these easy tips, hopefully you will be rewarded in growing grapes in your yard. After harvest time, you can do anything to your grape, turn it into a wine, dry it or turn it into preserves and sweets, just possibly anything that could make you happy and fulfilled! This book contains information on how to grow and maintain a grape garden.

Grape Growing History

Grape growing history is essentially dated ever since Neolithic periods and we really have proof that people were refining grapes then to create wines. It all began around 5 BC which last till today. Georgia is recognized to offer the oldest domestication of Vitis vinifera. While in 3200 BC there were numerous establishments which were dedicated to growing grapes.

Initially there were problems with male and female vine species due to pollination facts so Vitis vinifera, one hermaphrodite gender vine became well-liked. Hermaphrodite vines can simply pollinate themselves.

Viticulture practices were started during the time 1200 BC to 900 BC by the Phoenician. As time passed the techniques became really well-liked in Carthage. There is a twenty eight volume manuscript by a Carthaginian writer Mago which speaks about these viticulture routines in depth. This manuscript survived the large scale destruction of Carthage artifacts by the Roman Empire during the 3rd Punic War and gave valuable information on the history of grape growing.

Inspired by these scripts, Roman statesman Cato de Elder, wrote De Agra Cultura in 160 BC that described the viticulture as well as agriculture of the Romans. De Re Rustica, written by Columella, discussed lots regarding the Roman viticulture. The first ever mentioning of the use of trellils for grape wine support shown up in Columella writings.

He is also speaking about early trends that saw vines being trained to grow on several tree trunks as well as strategies that revolutionize everything with the use of stakes rather than tree trunks. Columella fundamentally liked stakes since it was truly challenging to prune vines when they were growing on trees. As vegetation thickness halted proper sunlight exposure for the vines pruning became essential.

World well known wine-growing regions such as the Spanish Rioja, the German Mosel, as well as the French Bordeaux, Burgundy and Rhone came into picture when Roman Empire spread into Western Europe making prominent their viticulture also.

Roman viticulturists stood out as pioneers when determining excellent locations to grow grapevines. They managed to realize that cold air is travelling downhill as well as comes from the valley's top. Grapevines were actually delicate while in cold environments and winter frost stood out as not truly suitable for numerous grapes.

Catholic monks were actually great viticulturists in the middle Ages. Vintage wines that were similar were developed because of the launch of cru vineyards. This was when Metayage system came out in France and grew to become quite famous. The laborers had the option of deciding most of the facts connected with viticulture from grape species to method of growing.

The middle age practices did last till around the 18th century. A bunch of research has been done to see match ups levels of certain grapevines with given places. During this time period we saw many conflicts related to quantity. The powerful and prosperous landlords preferred quality as it gave them good quality wines. Laborers did think about quantity too because this gave them additional money.

Grape growing history started around the year 5 BC and appeared in Europe because of the Roman Empire, which brought it from Greece. The vineyards modern day culture came out thanks to Catholic Monks. Various eras as well as many places have proof of viticulture being practiced since medieval times.

Grape Gardening

Grape vines yield not only delectable and varied grapes, but they also lend drama to a garden or landscape. They are fast-growing plants that, with careful pruning, can yield fruit in only a few years and live for 30 years or more!

Grapes are not only delicious for eating, juicing, and wine making, but they are also a lovely aesthetic plant to grow and harvest.

For home gardeners, there are three main types of grapes to consider: American (Vitis labrusca), European (V. vinifera), and French-American hybrids. American grapes are the most cold-hardy, while European grapes usually better for wine than the table do well in warm, dry, Mediterranean-type zones. Hybrids tend to be both cold-hardy and disease-resistant, but are not as flavorful as European grapes. Another type that is grown in the U.S. is the Muscadine (V. rotundifolia), which is native to the southern United States. The Muscadine grape's thick skin make it best suited for use in jams, wine, or other processed grape products.

Make sure the grape vines you buy are from a reputable nursery. The ideal plants are vigorous, one-year-old plants. 1-year-old plants that are smaller and occasionally weaker are sometimes held over by nurseries for another year of growth before being marketed as 2-year-old stock. If at all possible, obtain virus-free goods.

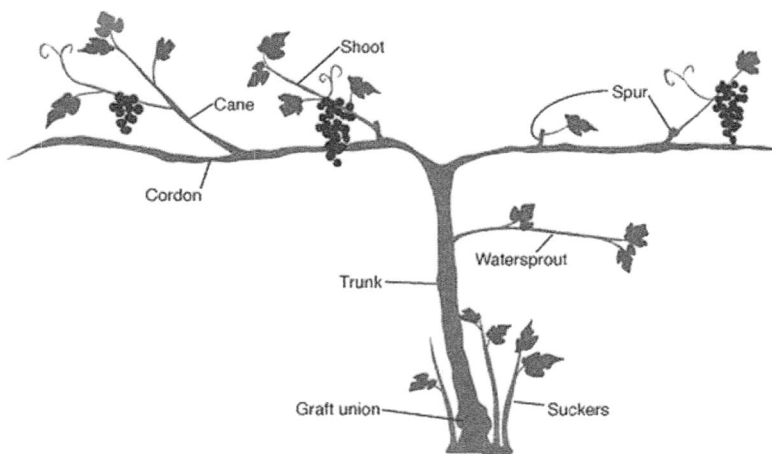

Overview of Grape Gardening

Grapevines thrive in full sun for 7 to 8 hours each day. Lower fruit output, decreased fruit quality, increased powdery mildew, and fruit rot all result from a lack of light.

Grapevines can grow and yield in a variety of soil types, but proper drainage is essential. Although most roots grow in the first three feet of soil, they can grow up to 15 feet deep. Soils should be at least 3 or 4 feet deep above hardpan, stratified layer, or rock, though 2 feet of soil can suffice with careful management.

The best wine quality often comes from vines that are grown on less fertile and rocky soils. Less fertile soils often produce smaller berries, which is preferable for winemaking because it gives a greater skin to juice ratio.

Large berries are desirable for table grapes, so deep and rich soils are preferred, although vegetative growth can be rampant. Table grapes also grow quite well on less fertile soils and the reduced vegetative growth may be less cumbersome.

Before planting, substantial amounts of well decomposed compost should be added into poorly drained soil. For each plant, deeply incorporate 2 inches of compost in an area up to 10 feet broad. Consider utilizing raised beds or planters that contain good soil if the soil is adobe clay or shallow hardpan.

There are 3 keys to growing grapes at home.

- Know the variety of grape you are growing and its growth habits.
- Know the ripening habits of the grape you are growing.
- Know if the variety provides the type of grape you want – i.e. table or wine.

The most frequent grapes to grow if you live east of the Rocky Mountains are Concord varieties. Concord kinds have a drooping growth tendency, which necessitates training them high and allowing them to droop. However, if you live west of the Rocky Mountains, the European varieties are the most common grapes to grow. The European kinds have a tendency to develop upwards, thus they must be trained low and allowed to stretch upwards. Different grape types have different harvest times, ranging from a few days to over 170 days, therefore it's crucial to grow a grape variety that will ripen in time for your area and conditions.

Also, consider which type of grape you'll want: table or wine. Table grapes are lower in sugar content and less acidic as they are meant to be eaten. Wine grapes are small and seedy with higher sugar and acid contents more suited to wine making..

How much space is needed

Spacing between rows can be as little as 8 ft. apart where soils are marginal and up to 12 ft. for wider trellis systems and deep, rich soils. Vine spacing within the row can be 6 to 9 ft. apart. A typical spacing might be 8 ft. apart to accommodate normal growth.

Grapes are frequently planted on arbors in the home. Use one vine per 50-100 square feet of space. arbor space of at least ft., or more if strong cultivars are utilized. A good vine will need at least 50 square feet of arbor space, while vigorous types or vines planted in deep, rich soil will need at least 75 square feet.

Nutritional Values of Grapes

- Calories 60
- Fat 0 g
- Cholesterol 0 mg
- Sodium 0 mg
- Carbohydrate 14 g
- Dietary Fiber 1 g
- Protein 1 g
- Vitamin A 2%
- Vitamin C 15%

- Iron 2%

Establishing Grape Gardening

Planting

- Plant dormant, bare-root grape vines in the early spring.
- Most grape varieties are self-fertile. To be sure, ask when you are buying vines if you will need more than one plant for pollination.
- Select a site with full sun. If you don't have a spot with full sun, make sure it at least gets morning sun. A small amount of afternoon shade won't hurt. Your soil needs to be deep, well-drained, and loose. You also need good air circulation.
- Grape vines will need to be trained to some sort of support to grow upward. This will also cut the risk of disease. The support needs to be in place at planting.
- A robust trellis or arbor is one option. Depending on whether the arbor is attached to

the home or another structure, it may have two, four, or six posts. The arbor can be held together with 2-inch by 4-inch wooden slats and topped with 1-inch by 2-inch wood pieces to form a lattice work for the vines to grow on. Corner bracing may be required to secure the entire building. One grape per post should be grown, with the strongest cane being chosen. Allow it to grow to the top of the post for the first year, then secure it as it matures.

- If you are low on free space, try growing grapes on a stake. Pound in a sturdy stake next to the grape vine and securely attach it. Keep the vine growing vertically. Let the vine grow to the top of the stake the first year then top it. Allow 4 to 5 side canes to grow. Remove all the rest.

- Before planting grapevines, soak their roots in water for two or three hours.

- Space vines 6 to 10 feet apart (16 feet for muscadines).

- Dig a planting hole 12 inches deep and 12 inches wide for each vine. Fill the container with 4 inches of topsoil. Remove any broken roots and plant the vine somewhat deeper in the hole than it grew in the nursery. 6 inches of earth should be used to cover the roots, and it should be tamped down. Fill up the rest of the hole with the remaining soil, but don't press it down.

- Water at time of planting.

Care

- Do not fertilize in the first year unless you have problem soil. Fertilize lightly in the second year of growth.
- Use mulch to keep an even amount of moisture around the vines.
- A mesh net is useful in keeping birds away from budding fruit.

Pruning Grapes

Pruning is a crucial part of the process. Grapes are produced on shoots that sprout from one-year-old canes. There will be less grapes if you have too many old canes (due to lack of pruning). If you thoroughly cut your vines each year, you'll receive a lot of new growth but few grapes.

Pruning takes place in late winter, around March, when the plant is dormant. The goal for the first year or so is to establish a strong root system and trunk. Plant the grape vine in the spring and cut it back to three buds. Then you'll have to wait till the first winter. If you're growing grapes on a trellis or arbor: One grape per post should be grown, with the strongest cane being chosen. Allow it to grow to the top of the post for the first year, then secure it as it matures. Top the cane and allow it to grow side branches along the top of the arbor the first winter. If you let the vines just continue to grow, they will produce dense shade, but little fruit. Prune the grapes each winter by removing those canes that fruited the previous year, cutting back one-year-old canes to five to six buds, and leaving some renewal canes pruned back to two to three buds. The goal is to have canes on the trellis spaced 2 to 3 feet apart. Remove any weak, thin canes. You want to leave enough fruiting canes on the trellis to fill it back in each summer, but not so many that is becomes a tangled mess.

If you're planting grapes on a stake, trim the side canes down to three buds apiece in the first winter. These will send forth branches the following year, which will produce grapes. Remove any weak or spindly growth, especially along the trunk's lower sections. In the second winter, prune the healthiest canes back to six to ten buds, pick two canes as renewal spurs and trim them back to three buds each, and remove the rest. This pruning should be done every winter. As your tree grows older, it should be able to support four to seven fruiting canes per year.

Harvest and Storage

- If grapes aren't ripening, pinch back some of the foliage to let in more sunlight.
- Grapes will not continue ripening once picked from the vine. Test a few to see if they are to

your liking before harvesting, usually in late summer or early fall.

- Grapes are ripe and ready to harvest when they are rich in color, juicy, full-flavored, easily crushed but not shriveled, and plump. They should be tightly attached to the stems. Sample different grapes from different clusters, and the taste should be between sweet and tart. Check our ripeness guide for more tips on color.
- Grapes can be stored in the cellar for up to six weeks, but keep them separate because they absorb the scents of other fruits and vegetables. Use clean, dry straw to line cardboard boxes or crates. Straw or sawdust can be used to separate the bunches. Check for spoiling on a regular basis.

Steps to Preparing a Grape Garden

Prepare the Site

Grape vines should be located in sites with well-drained sandy soil that receive full sun. Work at least 2" of organic soil conditioner into the top 10" of the planting site. Grape vines require a trellis or support system of some kind. As a general rule, each grapevine needs about 4' to 5' of trellis space. It's wise to position the trellis before planting the grape vines.

Plant the Vines

To keep the roots hydrated, soak the vines in a bucket of water. At the base of the trellis, dig a planting hole. If you're going to plant many vines, space the holes 5 to 8 feet apart. In the hole, plant the grape vine and fan out its roots. Backfill the hole with soil until it's three-quarters full, then water well to settle the soil. Finish filling the hole and water once more. Mulch around the vines.

Prune the Vines

Proper pruning techniques can make or break the success of a grape vine. After planting, prune the vine back to just one vigorous cane. The following spring, prune all but the most vigorous canes. Carefully tie the remaining canes to the trellis with twine. In future years, continue to keep only the most vigorous canes while pruning older, weaker ones.

Cultivate the Vines

Young vines need a fair amount of water while they are getting established. Drip irrigation is the best method since it prevents water from getting on the leaves, which can cause disease. For mature vines, too little water is better than too much water. In late spring, apply a slow-release 10-10-10 fertilizer around the plants but away from the stems.

Thin the Fruit

The first year, thin all the flower clusters that appear on the vines. This focuses the plant's energy on producing healthy leaves, branches and roots. In following years, thin flower clusters to just one or two per shoot. This provides more room for the remaining clusters to grow to full size.

Harvest the Grapes

The best way to tell when table grapes are ready for harvest is by tasting them. Grapes don't ripen after picking, so make sure they're fully ripe before harvesting them. For wine grapes, the use of a refractometer to test the fruit's sugar content may be necessary. The grapes should have between 18 and 22 percent sugar.

Suitable Soil Types

Having a working knowledge and understanding in geology, along with Pedology-study of soil and

Edaphology- the study of the influence of soil, is indispensable for the successful harvest of wine grapes and quality wine production. Selecting a soil for wine is tricky because the soil type needs to work for both the vine and the rootstock (a healthy underground part used for grafting and avoid damage). Soil influences the quality of the wine. It also affects the characteristics of wine grape through their supply of minerals and nutrients to grapevines. Hence it is necessary to understand the type of soil and its attributes which contribute to what we sense in a wine glass. A good soil type can be determined by its texture, depth, color, its organic composition, pH, drainage etc. Here is a brief outline of the primary soil types.

Sandy soil

Sandy soils are made of large particles, which are well-drained and retain heat. Because sand drains moderately which works well in wet climates but for regions with drought, sandy soils can be problematic.

A wine grown in warm climatic region is softer with less color, lighter acidity, and tannin. Whereas in cooler region, sandy soils retain heat and drain well to produce highly aromatic wines. Good thing is that this type of soil retains more heat and less moisture thus removing the possibility of diseases, but in some cases, it can also cause vine dehydration. Plus point of sandy soil is that it is resistant to the nasty louse phylloxera from attacking.

Regions with sandy soil: Bordeaux's Medoc and Graves

Clay soil

Clay soil is made up of small particles that hold water for longer periods of time. In harsh weather, the soil's ability to stay colder rises, which is beneficial to the grape vines. Clay soils retain moisture in hotter regions. These soils are known to produce world-class red and white wines that are robust and muscular.

Loam Soil

Most experts suggest loamy soil as the best type of soil for grape growing. A crumbly mix of sand, silt, and clay when blended with other soils in the right amounts offers the ideal soil type for grape growing. This is because the clay in loam drains well but contains a moderate amount of water and nutrients and generally lies within the preferred pH range.

Regions with loam soil: Sonoma Valley, Napa Valley

Volcanic Soil

Volcanic soil, as the name implies, is the consequence of a long-ago volcanic explosion. This fine-grained soil traps and maintains heat, drains efficiently, and holds water. Specific minerals such as iron, calcium, magnesium, and potassium are abundant in volcanic soil. Although not all volcanic soils are appropriate for producing vines, when specific conditions are met, the glass becomes magical. It is also supposed to give wines a rusty flavor.

Regions with volcanic soil: Sicily, Santorini

Limestone

Limestone is famous for quality winemaking, indeed, it is found in many famous regions. It is formed from the decomposed bodies of fish and other organic material which once lived in the ancient seabed. Limestone offers good drainage in wet weather but retains water in dry weather. It has high pH as it can reflect sunlight to promote photosynthesis. Wines made in limestone are long-lived and high acid wines.

Regions with limestone soil: Burgundy, Champagne

Silt soil

A silt soil has a fine texture than sand and is moderately porous. It has a good water retention property which is due to the small particles of soil, but this can also result in water logging, which can lead to vineyard disease. The wines are smooth and round with lesser acidity. Although some silt soils can be too fertile for quality winemaking, Loess is one good variety, which is a wind-blown type of silt with high proportions of silica.

Pests/Diseases and Control

Aphids

What are Aphids?

Aphids seems to infiltrate every garden. They are soft-bodied, tiny insects that subsist by sucking nutrient-rich liquids from plants. They can drastically weaken plants in huge numbers, causing damage to blooms and fruit. Aphids reproduce quickly, therefore it's critical to get them under control before they reproduce. In a single season, many generations can occur.

The good news is that they tend to move rather slowly and aphid control is relatively easy.

Identifying Aphids

Aphids are tiny (adults are under ¼-inch), and often nearly invisible to the naked eye. Various species can appear white, black, brown, gray, yellow, light green, or even pink! Some may have a waxy or woolly coating. They have pear-shaped bodies with long antennae; the nymphs look similar to adults. Most species have two short tubes (called cornicles) projecting from their hind end.

Adults are normally wingless, but most species can acquire wings when populations get overcrowded, allowing the insects to migrate to different plants, reproduce, and start a new colony if food quality worsens. Aphids normally eat in huge groups, though you may encounter them single or in small groups on occasion.

While aphids in general feed on a wide variety of plants, different species of aphids can be specific to certain plants. For example, some species include bean aphids, cabbage aphids, potato aphids, green peach aphids, melon aphids, and woolly apple aphids. Some aphids are darker colors, like brown. The potato aphid is a common brown aphid. Photo credit: GrowVeg.com.

What does Aphid damage looks like?

- Nymphs and adults feed on plant juices, attacking leaves, stems, buds, flowers, fruit, and/or roots, depending on the species. Most aphids especially like succulent new growth. Some, such as the green peach aphid, feed on a variety of plants, while others, such as the rosy apple aphid, focus on one or just a few plant hosts.
- Look for misshapen, curling, stunted, or yellowing leaves. Be sure to check the undersides of leaves; aphids love to hide there.
- If the leaves or stems are covered with a sticky substance, that is a sign that aphids may have been sipping sap. This "honeydew," a sugary liquid produced by the insects as waste, can attract other insects, such as ants, which gather the substance for food. When aphids feed on

trees, their honeydew can drop onto cars, outdoor furniture, driveways, and so on.

- The honeydew can sometimes encourage a fungal growth called sooty mold, causing branches and leaves to appear black.
- Flowers or fruit can become distorted or deformed due to feeding aphids.
- Some aphid species cause galls to form on roots or leaves.
- Aphids may transmit viruses between plants, and also attract other insects that prey on them, such as ladybugs.

How to control Aphids

- Try spraying cold water on the leaves; sometimes all aphids need is a cool blast to dislodge them. Typically they are unable to find their way back to the same plant.
- If you have a large aphid invasion, dust plants with flour. It constipates the pests.

- Neem oil, insecticidal soaps, and horticultural oils are effective against aphids. Be sure to follow the application instructions provided on the packaging.
- You can often get rid of aphids by wiping or spraying the leaves of the plant with a mild solution of water and a few drops of dish soap. Soapy water should be reapplied every 2-3 days for 2 weeks.
- One variation of this soap-water mix includes cayenne pepper: Stir together 1 quart water, 1 tsp liquid dish soap, and a pinch of cayenne pepper. Do not dilute before spraying on plants.
- Diatomaceous earth (DE) is a non-toxic, organic material that will kill aphids. Do not apply DE when plants are in bloom; it is harmful to pollinators, too.

How to prevent Aphids

- For fruit or shade trees, spray dormant horticultural oil to kill overwintering aphid eggs.
- Aphids will be eaten by beneficial insects such as ladybugs, lacewings, and parasitic wasps. Additional populations of these insects can be acquired online, which should assist keep aphid populations under control right now.
- Companion planting can be very helpful to keep aphids away from your plants in the first place. For example:
- Aphids are repelled by catnip.
- Aphids are especially attracted to mustard and nasturtium. Plant these near more valuable plants as traps for the aphids. (Check your trap plants regularly to keep aphid populations from jumping to your valued plants.)
- Nasturtiums spoil the taste of fruit tree sap for aphids and will help keep aphids off of broccoli.
- Garlic and chives repel aphids when planted near lettuce, peas, and rose bushes.

- getting-rid-of-aphids_full_width.jpg
- Hosing down your plants is one way to control the aphid population in your garden.

Using Alcohol to prevent Aphids

Isopropyl alcohol (also called isopropanol or rubbing alcohol) works fine and is easy to find, but be sure it doesn't have additives. Ethanol (grain alcohol) seems to work best. Alcohol usually comes in 70 percent strength in stores (or 95 percent strength purchased commercially). To make an insecticidal spray, mix equal parts 70 percent alcohol and water (or, if using 95 percent alcohol, mix 1 part alcohol to 1 ½ parts water).

You can also add alcohol to a soapy emulsion to make it more effective. For example, in a spray bottle, combine 5 cups water, 2 cups alcohol, and 1 tablespoon liquid soap.

Caution: When applying an alcohol or soap spray, or a combination, always test a small area first, and apply in morning or evening, when the sun is not beating down. Watch the plant for a few days for any adverse reactions before applying more. Plants can be sensitive to alcohol and soap. Also, some soaps have additives that can damage plants—select the purest form.

Japanese Beetles

What are Japanese Beetles?

Japanese beetles (Popillia japonica) are small insects that carry a big threat. They do not discriminate when it comes to what types of plants they feed on, though they do have favorites (like roses). In fact, they are classified as a pest to hundreds of different species. They are one of the major insect pests in the Eastern and Midwestern United States, causing monumental damage to crops each year.

Prior to the beetle's accidental introduction to the United States in the early 1900s, the Japanese beetle was found only on the islands of Japan, isolated by water and kept in check by its natural predators. In 1912, a law was passed that made it illegal to import plants rooted in soil. Unfortunately, the failure to implement the law immediately allowed the Japanese beetle to arrive in this country. Most entomologists agree that the beetles entered the country as grubs in soil on Japanese iris roots. In 1916, these coppery-winged pests were first spotted in a nursery near Riverton, New Jersey, and by 1920, eradication programs were dropped; the beetle proved to be too prolific and widespread.

How to identify Japanese Beetles:

• Japanese Beetles are ½ inch in length with metallic blue-green heads, copper-colored backs, tan wings, and small white hairs lining each side of the abdomen. Japanese beetles usually feed in small groups. They lay eggs in the soil during June, which develop into tiny white grubs with brown heads and six legs that are up to ¾ inch in length. These grubs will remain underground for about 10 months, overwintering and growing in the soil.

• They emerge from the soil as adult beetles in June and begin feasting. Plants are frequently attacked in groups, which is why the damage is so severe. The adult Japanese beetle has a short life cycle of about 40 days, yet it can traverse a lot of land. Even if you manage to keep your Japanese beetle population under control, your neighbors' Japanese beetles may invade.

Signs of Japanese Beetles:

• Japanese beetles feed on a wide variety of flowers and crops (the adult beetles attack more than 300 different kinds of plants), but in terms of garden plants, they are especially common on roses, as well as beans, grapes, and raspberries. Here's what to look out for:

• Japanese beetles can devour most of the foliage on favored plants, as well as the flowers. Look for leaves that are "skeletonized" (i.e., only have veins remaining). This is a tell-tale sign of Japanese beetles. (Mexican Bean Beetles can also leave foliage skeletonized, though, so be sure to identify the beetle by their appearance as well.) Japanese beetles are not usually far from damaged leaves, so inspect the plant thoroughly. Also keep an eye on the ground beneath the plant; the beetles may reflexively drop off the plant if disturbed.

• Japanese beetle grubs damage grass when overwintering in the soil, as they feast on the roots of lawn grasses and garden plants. This can cause brown patches of dead or dying grass to form in the lawn, which will pull up easily thanks to the weakened roots.

How to control Japanese Beetles

Good horticultural practices, including watering and fertilizing, will reduce the impact of the damage caused by these beetles, but oftentimes you simply need to get rid of them. Here are some ideas:

• Row Covers: Protect your plants from Japanese beetles with row covers during the 6- to 8-week feeding period that begins in mid- to late May in the southern U.S. and in mid- to late June in the North. Row covers will keep the pests out, but they will keep pollinators out, too; be sure to remove them if your crops need to be pollinated.

• Hand Pick: Unfortunately, handpicking Japanese beetles from plants is the most efficient approach to get rid of them. It takes time, but it pays off, especially if you are persistent. Pick them up and place them in a solution of 1 tablespoon liquid dishwashing detergent and water, where they will drown.

• Neem Oil: Neem oil and sprays containing potassium bicarbonate are somewhat effective, especially on roses. The adult beetles ingest a chemical in the neem oil and pass it on in their eggs, and the resulting larvae die before they become adults. Note: Neem can be harmful to fish and other aquatic life, so don't use it near lakes, rivers, and ponds. It must be reapplied after rain.

• Use a Dropcloth: Put down a dropcloth and, in the early morning when the beetles are most active, shake them off and dump them into a bucket of soapy water.

• Insecticides: If you wish to spray or dust with insecticides, speak to your local cooperative extension or garden center about approved insecticides in your area.

Or, try this homemade solution: Mix 1 teaspoon of liquid dishwashing detergent with 1 cup of vegetable oil and shake well; then add it to 1 quart of water. Add 1 cup of rubbing alcohol and shake vigorously to emulsify. Pour this mixture into a spray bottle and use it at ten-day intervals on pests.

Warning: Homemade sprays can run more of a risk of damaging plant leaves, so be careful and use sparingly. It's always a good idea to first test a little bit of your spray on a small part of your plant, wait 24 hours to see if there are any adverse reactions, and if not proceed with spraying the rest of the plant.

Apply sprays in the morning, never in full sun or at temperatures above 90°F. If your plants start to wilt, rinse the leaves immediately with clean water.

• Japanese Beetle Traps: Japanese beetle traps can be helpful in controlling large numbers of beetles, but they also might attract beetles from beyond your yard. Eugenol and geraniol, aromatic chemicals extracted from plants, are attractive to adult Japanese beetles as well as to other insects. Unfortunately, the traps do not effectively suppress adults and might even result in a higher localized population. If you want to try them, be sure to place traps far away from target plants so that the beetles do not land on your favored flowers and crops on their way to the traps.

• Fruit Cocktail Trap: You can buy a variety of Japanese beetle traps, but most of them are about as effective as a can of fruit cocktail. Open the can and leave it to ferment for a week in the sun. Then, in a light-colored pail, lay it on top of bricks or wood blocks, and fill the pail with water to just below the top of the can. Place the bucket about 25 feet away from the plants that need to be protected. Beetles will flock to the tasty bait, fall into the water, and drown. Start anew if the bait becomes diluted due to rain.

• Geraniums: Japanese beetles are attracted to geraniums. They eat the blossoms, promptly get dizzy from the natural chemicals in the geranium, fall off the plant, and permit you to dispose of them conveniently with a dustpan and brush. Plant geraniums close to more valuable plants which you wish to save from the ravages of Japanese beetles.

Japanese Beetles on Roses? Note that insecticides will not fully protect roses, which unfold too fast and are especially attractive to beetles. When beetles are most abundant on roses, nip the buds and spray the bushes to protect the leaves. When the beetles become scarce, let the bushes bloom again. Timeliness and thoroughness of application are very important. Begin treatment as soon as beetles appear, before damage is done.

How to prevent Japanese Beetles

Unfortunately, there is no magic potion to get rid of this pest. For general preventive maintenance, experts recommend keeping your landscape healthy. Remove diseased and poorly nourished trees as well as any prematurely ripening or diseased fruits, which can attract Japanese beetles. Try these tips:

• Choose the Right Plants: Select plants that Japanese beetles will not be attracted to. See our list of the Best and Worst Plants for Japanese Beetles. Dispersing their favorite plants throughout the landscape, rather than grouping them together, can also help.

• Get Rid of Grubs: In the grub stage of late spring and fall (beetles have two life cycles per season), spray the lawn with 2 tablespoons of liquid dishwashing soap diluted in 1 gallon of water per 1,000 square feet. The grubs will surface and the birds will love you. Spray once each week until no more grubs surface.

• Milky Spore: To control the population of Japanese beetle larvae, you can introduce the fungal illness milky spore into your grass. The spores are consumed by the grubs as they forage in the soil. This strategy only works if the spore count has been raised for two to three years. Fortunately, the spores can survive for years in the soil. This is a costly treatment because every soil within five-eighths of a mile must be treated for effective control.

• Beneficial Nematodes: You can also drench sod with parasitic nematodes to control the larvae. The nematodes must be applied when the grubs are small and if the lawn is irrigated before and after application. Preparations containing the Heterorhabditis species seem to be most effective.

• Plant Strategically: Companion planting can be a useful strategy in preventing pests. Try planting garlic, rue, or tansy near your affected plants to deter Japanese beetles.

• Parasitic Wasps: You can also attract native species of parasitic wasps (Tiphia vernalis or T. popilliavora) and flies to your garden, as they are predators of the beetles and can be beneficial insects. They will probably attack the larvae, but they are not very effective in reducing the overall beetle population.

Warning: Honeybees, native bees, and other pollinators are very hazardous to many dusts and sprays. If these products must be applied to plants during the bloom period, do not do it during hours when bees are visiting the flowers (late morning through mid-day). If you want to treat more than a few yard and garden plantings, you should call local beekeepers ahead of time so that they can safeguard their colonies.

Wondering about that white fungus on your plant? The fungal disease powdery mildew is a common problem in gardens, infecting a wide variety of plants and reducing the quality and quantity of flowers and fruit.

Powdery Mildew

What is Powdery Mildew?

Powdery mildew is a fungal disease that affects a wide variety of plants. There are many different species of powdery mildew, and each species attacks a range of different plants. In the garden, commonly affected plants include cucurbits (squash, pumpkins, cucumbers, melons), nightshades (tomatoes, eggplants, peppers), roses, and legumes (beans, peas).

A layer of mildew made up of many spores grows on the top of the leaves when the fungus begins to take over one of your plants. The wind then carries these spores to neighboring plants. Powdery mildew can stifle your plant's growth and, if the infection is serious enough, impair fruit yield and quality.

How does it spread?

• Powdery mildew spores typically drift into your garden with the wind, but if you've had powdery mildew occur in the past, new outbreaks may also come from dormant spores in old vegetative material or weeds nearby.

• Unlike many other fungal diseases, powdery mildew thrives in warm (60-80°F / 15-27°C), dry climates, though it does require fairly high relative humidity (i.e., humidity around the plant) to spread. In cooler, rainy areas, it does not spread as well, and it is also slowed down by temperatures higher than 90°F

(32°C). It tends to affect plants in shady areas more than those in direct sun, too.

How to identify

- Plants infected with powdery mildew look as if they have been dusted with flour.
- Powdery mildew usually starts off as circular, powdery white spots, which can appear on leaves, stems, and sometimes fruit.
- Powdery mildew usually covers the upper part of the leaves, but may grow on the undersides as well.
- Young foliage is most susceptible to damage. Leaves turn yellow and dry out.
- The fungus might cause some leaves to twist, break, or become disfigured.
- The white spots of powdery mildew will spread to cover most of the leaves or affected areas.
- The leaves, buds, and growing tips will become disfigured as well. These symptoms usually appear late in the growing season.

- Powdery mildew first appears as small white spots on the upper part of the leaves. Photo Credit: The Regents of the University of California, UC Davis.

How to prevent powdery mildew:

• The best way to control powdery mildew, like all pests and diseases, is to prevent it. Powdery mildew-resistant plants are ideal for your landscape. Many mildew-resistant cucurbit cultivars (melons, cucumbers, squash, and so on) have been produced and are available from major seed companies.

• Plant in sunnier spots, as powdery mildew tends to develop more often in shady areas.

• Selectively prune overcrowded areas to increase air circulation around your plants; this helps to reduce relative humidity.

• Watering from overhead can help to wash spores off leaves. Note, however, that wet foliage can often contribute to the development of other common diseases, so it's best not to rely on this as a prevention tactic.

How to control:

• Consider spraying infected plants with protectant (preventative) fungicides. Effective organic fungicides for treating powdery mildew include sulfur, lime-sulfur, neem oil, and potassium bicarbonate. These are most effective when used prior to infection or when you first see signs of the disease.

• If you don't want to use chemical fungicides, try spraying your plants with a bicarbonate solution:

• Mix 1 teaspoon baking soda in 1 quart of water. Spray plants thoroughly, as the solution will only kill fungus that it comes into contact with.

• Because it's tough to get rid of the illness once plants are badly afflicted, concentrate on preventing it from spreading to other plants. Remove all sick foliage, stems, and fruit from the plant and dispose of it in the garbage or burn it. Remember that any affected plant should not be composted, as the illness can still be spread by the wind and persist in the composted materials.

Black Rot

Black rot, caused by the fungus Guignardia bidwellii, is a serious disease of cultivated and wild grapes. The disease is most destructive in warm, wet seasons. It attacks all green parts of the vine leaves, shoots, leaf and fruit stems, tendrils, and fruit. The most damaging effect is to the fruit.

Warm, muggy weather in the spring and summer, along with vulnerable types' fruit that hasn't been sprayed, can cause fruit to rot almost completely by harvest time. If sound cultural practices are followed combined with the application of preventative fungicide sprays, black rot is not difficult to control.

Symptoms and Diagnosis

• Leaves: Reddish brown and circular to angular spots appear on the upper surface of the leaves starting in late spring. As spots merge, they form irregular, reddish brown blotches. The number of spots or lesions per leaf varies from 2 to more than 100 depending on the severity of the disease. The center of the leaf spot turns tannish brown and is surrounded by a black margin. Black, speck-sized fruiting bodies (pycnidia) are arranged in a definite ring just inside the margin of the lesion. Only young, rapidly growing leaves are affected.

• Fruit: Shortly after the flower petals fall, fruit infection can occur. Most infections start when the fruit is half to almost full size. A small spot will appear that becomes circular and whitish tan, often surrounded by a brown ring. This happens while the berry is still green. The spots grow rapidly and may cover half of the berry within 48 hours. Within a few days the entire berry becomes coal black, hard, and mummified. The surface of the withered fruit is soon covered with minute, black, pimple-like, sporeproducing pycnidia that are arranged in circular zones.

Life Cycle

The black rot fungus overwinters in canes, tendrils, and leaves on the grape vine and on the ground. Mummified berries on the ground or those that are still clinging to the vines become the major infection source the following spring. During rain, microscopic spores (ascospores) are shot out of numerous, black fruiting bodies (perithecia) and are carried by air currents to young, expanding leaves. In the presence of moisture, these spores germinate in 36 to 48 hours and eventually penetrate the leaves and fruit stems. The infection becomes visible after 8 to 25 days. When the weather is wet, spores can be released the entire spring and summer providing continuous infection. Cool weather slows growth of the fungus. It requires warm weather for optimal growth and a period of 2 to 3 days of rain, drizzle, or fog.

New black rot infections continue into late spring and summer during prolonged periods of warm, rainy weather. During August, the pycnidia are transformed into the overwintering stage (pycnosclerotia) that gives rise to perithecia within which the spring ascospores are produced, completing the disease cycle.

Integrated Pest Management Strategies

Planting

Properly space vines and find a planting location where they will be exposed to full sun and have sufficient air circulation. Keep the vines off the ground and properly knotted, limiting the amount of time the vines are wet and so lowering the risk of infection.

Sanitation

Keep the fruit planting and surrounding areas free of weeds and tall grass. This practice will promote lower relative humidity and rapid drying of vines and thereby limit fungal infection.

Pruning

Prune the vines in early winter during dormancy. Select only a few strong, healthy canes from the previous year's growth to produce the following season's crop. Remove these prunings from the vineyard and burn or destroy.

Cultivation

Cultivate the vineyard before budbreak to bury the mummified berries. Diseased berries covered with soil do not produce spores that will reach the developing vines. For homegrown grapes, use 2–3 inches of leaf mulch or fine bark to cover infected debris.

Fungicides

Use protective fungicide sprays. Pesticides registered to protect the developing new growth include copper, captan, ferbam, mancozeb, maneb, triadimefon, and ziram. Important spraying times are as new shoots are 2 to 4 inches long, and again when they are 10 to 15 inches long, just before bloom, just after bloom, and when the fruit has set.

Cultivars

Cultivars with large, juicy berries are the most susceptible. In general, grapes that ripen late in the season are affected the least. Most commercial cultivars are sufficiently resistant if adequately protected with a fungicide spray program.

CONCLUSION

It takes time and effort, but you can see, growing grapes is not as complicated as it seems. Find out the specific requirements for the variety of grape you want to grow, and in the next two years, you could be harvesting your own juicy grapes!

Printed in Great Britain
by Amazon